under wraps

Also by Robert Chafe

Afterimage
Oil & Water
Robert Chafe: Two Plays (*Butler's Marsh*
    & *Tempting Providence*)

under wraps

A SPOKE OPERA

Robert Chafe

PLAYWRIGHTS CANADA PRESS

TORONTO

For professional or amateur production rights, please contact:
Ian Arnold, Catalyst Talent Creative Management
310-100 Broadview Ave., Toronto, ON M4M 3H3
416.645.0935, info@catalysttcm.com

LIBRARY AND ARCHIVES CANADA CATALOGUING IN PUBLICATION
Chafe, Robert, author
        Under wraps / Robert Chafe.

A play.
Issued in print and electronic formats.
ISBN 978-1-77091-251-9 (pbk.).--ISBN 978-1-77091-252-6
(pdf).--ISBN 978-1-77091-253-3 (epub)

        I. Title.

PS8555.H2655U53 2014   C812'.54   C2014-904095-4
                                            C2014-904096-2

We acknowledge the financial support of the Canada Council for the Arts, the Ontario Arts Council (OAC), the Ontario Media Development Corporation, and the Government of Canada through the Canada Book Fund for our publishing activities.

with thanks to B

Introduction

I first met Robert Chafe in the summer of 1996. I was six years into a decade-long sojourn on Canada's east coast, a CFA ("Come From Away") from Toronto who had just moved from Corner Brook, Newfoundland, to Charlottetown, Prince Edward Island. As one of two dramaturgs brought in by the Playwrights Atlantic Resource Centre (PARC) to facilitate its annual Moveable Feast playwrights' colony, luck dealt me a decidedly winning hand. One of the writers I was paired with was a young man from St. John's named Robert Chafe, who had submitted a lovely piece of writing entitled *Silent Partner*. On reading the text, prior to meeting Robert, I encountered a script that was smart, nuanced, and very funny—a contemporary gay turn on a time-tested romantic scenario of unrequited love at first sight. I remember what struck me first about it was how remarkably light on its feet it was, how nimbly it navigated traditional territory with constant, deceivingly subtle innovation. Which is another way of saying that what impressed me is the quality I appreciate most about a successful drama: how it *moves*. The result was, and remains, somehow, quietly startling.

And then I met Robert.

Rarely are the best qualities of a piece of writing so reflective of its author. Truly, the phrase "quietly startling" is just as appropriate for the man as it is for the text. My first impression—of a rare combination of self-deprecating humility, deep intelligence, and burning courage—has remained strong and consistent throughout the nearly two decades I have called Robert my friend. It became clear immediately that the script was highly personal—indeed, autobiographical—and that its author similarly resided firmly at the intersection of comic agility and deep conviction.

And then I discovered Artistic Fraud of Newfoundland.

No doubt my most vivid memory of our original work on the script that would become *Under Wraps* was when Robert began to explain how it would be performed. As he introduced (*in abstensia*) his collaborators—foremost among them director Jillian Keiley and composer Petrina Bromley—and he began to describe the elaborate and painstakingly precise process that Jill calls Kaliedography, I quickly moved from an initial state of confusion to one of surprising clarity. Eighteen actor/singers, moving blindly beneath a 40' X 60' parachute cloth, hitting their marks on a mathematically structured floor grid, thereby continuously creating and recreating the physical and sonic environment of the production? It was not until I saw the touring production in Halifax, over a year later, that I fully understood and appreciated the complexity of the piece's vision. Yet, somehow, all these elements are present and accounted for in the grace, wit, and oh-so-beating heart of this nimble text.

As anyone who follows Canadian theatre knows, Robert, Jill, and their collaborators at Artistic Fraud have accomplished much in the years since *Under Wraps* was first uncovered. The play, the first for the company to tour beyond Newfoundland, was followed by a succession of equally groundbreaking projects. Winner of a Governor General's Literary Award for Drama (in 2010 for *Afterimage*), Robert has emerged as one of this country's most accomplished and celebrated playwrights. But there is no question *Under Wraps* remains as vital as any of his pieces, and as deeply personal for its author. Last year, in the lead up to a highly successful remount in St. John's, I had the pleasure of revisiting the dramaturgical process on the text with Robert, with the benefit of almost twenty years of retrospection to draw upon. One result is this gently but effectively revised version of a delightful, supple, and wise treatise on hope and desire. At the same time, I was reminded, often poignantly, of just how close to the bone and to the heart Robert carries this piece. It might also be said, by extension, that this piece carries part of Robert to every reader, to every spectator. For that reason alone, this publication, in 2014, is nothing short of a cause for celebration.

—Bruce Barton, summer 2014

Under Wraps premiered on February 12, 1997, at the LSPU Hall in St. John's with the following cast and creative team:

Mark: Robert Chafe
David: Steve Cochrane
Chorus: Jennifer Adams, Selina Asgar, Neil Butler, Alison Carter, Diana Daly, Philip Goodridge, Gina Granter, Allan Hawco, Denise Hennebury, Danielle Irvine, Tonya Kearley, Thea Morash, Jerry Stamp, Anna Stassis, Jon Weir, and Erin Whitney

Directed and designed by Jillian Keiley
Music composition and direction by Petrina Bromley
Lighting design by Geoff Seymour Jr.
Stage management by Kelly Jones
Assistant stage management by Heather Crossan

Artistic Fraud remounted the show and toured it to Eastern Front Theatre in Halifax (February 17–21, 1999); the High Performance Rodeo in Calgary (January 7–11, 2000); and the Vancouver East Cultural Centre, in association with Rumble Productions (January 25–29, 2000), with the following company:

Mark: Robert Chafe
David: Steve Cochrane
Chorus: Neil Butler, Alison Butt, Alison Carter, Pam Correstine, Diana Daly, Philip Goodridge, Lawrence Haegert, Chris Harnett, Jonny Harris, Denise Hennebury, Danielle Irvine, Willow Kean, Tonya Kearley, Leah Lewis, James McAndrew, Thea Morash, Sean Panting, Tanya Penney, Jane Peters, Steve Pretty, Nicole Rousseau, Carolyn Staple, Anna Stassis, and Erin Whitney

Artistic Fraud redeveloped the show and premiered the new version on May 8, 2013, at the LSPU Hall in St. John's with the following cast and creative team:

Mark: Ron Klappholz
David: Greg Gale
Chorus: Brad Bonnell, Petrina Bromley, Courtney Brown, Robert Chafe, Victoria Harnett, Marie Jones, Willow Kean, Justin Nurse, Mark Power, Michael Power, Anna Stassis, Jeremy Wells, Mark White, and Alison Woolridge

Directed and designed by Jillian Keiley
Musical direction by Petrina Bromley
Lighting design by Leigh Ann Vardy
Stage management by Kai-Yueh Chen
Assistant stage management by Mark Denine
Piano by Wade Tarling

Note on Production

Under Wraps was conceived by its director, Jillian Keiley, as a "spoken opera." The actors playing Mark and David timed the delivery of their lines to align with Petrina Bromley's constant score, creating a hybrid of naturalistically spoken text and piano/vocal music. Chorus lines were sometimes spoken individually by a single chorus member, but more often than not were sung in full harmony as a line in the music. The chorus themselves were blanketed under a 60' x 40' white parachute cloth. While providing score and auxiliary text, they manipulated this fabric to form settings for the two lead actors on top of the sheet.

Characters

Mark
David

Act 1

MARK and DAVID enter from opposite sides of the stage and cross towards each other. When they become aware of one another they immediately slow down and grow very tense. As they pass, MARK weakly looks up.

MARK   Hey.

DAVID continues on his way without acknowledging MARK. MARK slows to a stop.

I am... completely... invisible.

The lights come up to full as the CHORUS booms in.

CHORUS   Yes you are.

DAVID   I don't see anybody. Hello? Hello?

MARK   August 22, 2009. My birthday. That's when it happened.

DAVID   Hello?

MARK   I remember it like it was yesterday. The first time I saw that face.

DAVID   Is there anybody here?

MARK   I was wearing this shirt. I was in a really good place in my life.

DAVID   Hello? Anybody?

MARK   I was still sporting a size thirty-four pant.

DAVID   The front door was open so...

MARK   Do we hunt out memories or do they hunt out us?

DAVID   Hello?

MARK   His name was David.

CHORUS   Enter Dave.

DAVID   Hello?

CHORUS   Is there anybody there?

MARK   Hello?

CHORUS   Is there somebody here?

DAVID   Hello.

CHORUS   Hello.

MARK   Hello.

CHORUS   I love you.

           MARK looks at us.

MARK   I worked in a furniture store.

           The CHORUS form a furniture store.

DAVID   I'm here about the job.

MARK   We were hiring. Only two days and there was a stack of resumés on my desk higher than a small dog.

           The job?

DAVID   Yeah. Yeah, I saw the ad here in *The Telegram*.

           MARK is playing it too cool.

MARK   *The Telegram.*

           DAVID is unsure of what to say or do.

           Okay, so I was a little more reserved back then. Some would say "shy." Some would say "withdrawn." Some would say "desperately in the closet."

DAVID   It's not gone already, is it? Oh man, I knew I should have come down yesterday. But no. Priorities. I gotta get my priorities straight. The haircut could have waited. I could have visited Nan next week. I could have...

MARK   He was a talker. His little pink tongue wagging and waving. He had a really kind voice. But that wasn't it. He was all nervous and nice. But that wasn't it either. At first, I thought it was completely physical.

CHORUS Those eyes.

MARK *is looking at everything but his haircut.*

MARK   That great haircut.

CHORUS That smile.

MARK   But that couldn't be it completely. I mean, he was a fantasy made flesh, sure, but that was a pretty guarded fantasy, m'kay. And yet here I was, all overcome like a fat kid at a fish fry.

CHORUS So?

MARK   So what was it with this guy? In retrospect, I can boil it all down to two things.

CHORUS Two things...

MARK   ...that were completely unrelated to his physique.

CHORUS Two things...

MARK   ...that made me think that he might be the best thing since low-fat sour cream.

CHORUS One.

MARK He was, what, twenty-six years old and he still visited his grandmother. Sensitive. I could melt.

CHORUS Two.

MARK He had no fear of cursing during a job interview.

DAVID Shit!

MARK Balls. Dude had balls.

DAVID I should have come sooner.

MARK I should have come out right then and there.

DAVID Just my luck. I'll leave.

CHORUS I love you.

DAVID Pardon?

MARK I said...

I said the job has not been filled.

DAVID No?

MARK No. No, not yet. But I mean we... we have many... intriguing possibilities. Your resumé?

DAVID Oh yeah.

MARK Yes. Yes. David Sparkes?

DAVID   Dave.

MARK   Dave.

        They shake hands.

CHORUS   What a beautiful name.

MARK   Dave. Yes, of course. Let's just see if everything is in order here... Dave. Your schooling, experience, references.

CHORUS   Address, telephone number, marital status.

MARK   Yes.

CHORUS   Single!

MARK   Everything appears to be in order here, Dave.

DAVID   Great.

MARK   I just have to ask you a few questions.

DAVID   Shoot.

MARK   Ah... have you ever sold furniture before?

DAVID   No.

CHORUS   No.

MARK   Oh, okay—do have sales experience? Clothing retail?

DAVID   No.

CHORUS   No!

MARK   Um, a record store?

DAVID   No.

CHORUS   No!!

MARK   Grocery store?

DAVID   No.

CHORUS   No!!!

MARK   Convenience store?

DAVID   No.

CHORUS   No!!!!

MARK   Dave, have you ever worked anywhere where you had to see, and maybe even speak, to another person, another living person?

DAVID   I work as a lifeguard during the summer.

CHORUS   Yes!

MARK   People?

DAVID   Lots of them.

CHORUS   Yes!

MARK   Then you're our man!

DAVID   I am?

CHORUS   Yes!

MARK   You... you sure are.

DAVID   Man, this is my lucky day.

MARK   Mine too.

DAVID   What?

MARK   My birthday. Today.

DAVID   Oh, happy birthday.

MARK   Beauty, brains, and considerate too.

DAVID   So when do I start?

MARK   When do you start?

DAVID   Yeah.

CHORUS   When *do* you start?

MARK   You start... just as soon as I check it out with the boss.

DAVID   The boss? That means an interview, right?

MARK   Shy?

DAVID   No. I just get really stupid when I'm nervous.

MARK   Just a formality, Dave. Nothing to worry about. With your...

CHORUS   Eyes.

MARK   ...skills and your...

CHORUS   Ass.

MARK   ...pleasant demeanour, I'm sure that he's just... just going to love you.

DAVID   Yeah?

MARK   We'll be in touch, Dave.

DAVID   Thanks. Thanks a lot... ah...

MARK   Mark.

CHORUS   Happy birthday to me.

DAVID   Mark. Yeah, thanks.

MARK   No, Dave, thank you.

CHORUS   I love you.

MARK   Goodbye.

CHORUS   I am totally in love with you.

DAVID   Goodbye.

CHORUS   Later.

        And DAVID is gone.

MARK   Just like that.

CHORUS   That's how it happened.

MARK   One day you are completely disinterested in every other human being on the face of the planet, and...

MARK &
CHORUS   ...the next...

        MARK drops to his knees as the CHORUS form a rippling blue sea.

MARK   You're ready to throw yourself in front of a train because of someone you met in a furniture store.

CHORUS   A furniture store!

MARK   I took that job so I wouldn't have to meet people. I knew the dangers, the pitfalls of the modern workplace. Work in a bar—yeah right, and what?

CHORUS   I fall in love.

MARK   I work in a library…

CHORUS   I fall in love.

MARK   I plant trees in the outback of British Columbia, miles away from the nearest town, and…

CHORUS   I fall in love.

MARK   No! No. This here was different. This was a furniture store. Don't try to hide from the world, I said. Be proactive, I said. Get out there and surround yourself with the opposite of sexy.

CHORUS   A furniture store.

MARK   People of Walmart. Twenty-five kids apiece.

CHORUS   Polyester.

MARK   We weren't selling Ikea, folks. No Italian leather in this place. Only the ugliest assortment of household appointments this side of a seventies sitcom. Who'd even shop online at this place, I thought. I was safe here, I thought. I thought I had locked the door to physical temptation for good, and then who should find the key and just let himself in but...

CHORUS   David Sparkes.

MARK   David Sparkes.

CHORUS   David Sparkes, who was promised a job.

MARK   Shit!

The CHORUS *form a high curtain downstage. A solitary* CHORUS *figure emerges through the centre.*

CHORUS   A question of morals.

The curtains part to reveal MARK *donning a* CHORUS-*made cloak, looking dramatic.*

MARK　There was a stack of at least sixty resumés on my desk.

CHORUS　Sixty resumés.

MARK　University graduates all. Practical experience.

CHORUS　Sixty resumés.

MARK　And from those sixty resumés Mr. Wagner had to choose a lifeguard with no practical experience and an unfinished degree in philosophy.

CHORUS　He has to?

MARK　Sure. I promised, right?

CHORUS　Lied.

MARK　I promised. And I may be many many things, many despicable things, but I am not a liar. In most senses of the word.

CHORUS　Lied.

MARK　I promised. So what could I do? Call up the eighth wonder of the world and tell him that he was still unemployed?

CHORUS　Or...

MARK　Or, I accidentally misplace the stack.

CHORUS　Yes.

MARK　It just... just goes missing.

CHORUS   Yes.

MARK   I don't know, Mr. Wagner sir. It was there last night. I don't know what could have happened to it.

CHORUS   Yes.

MARK   What a shame, Wilson. All those fine candidates. Oh well, I guess we'll have to go with the lifeguard.

CHORUS   David Sparkes.

MARK   If you think that's best, sir.

CHORUS   Dave.

MARK   Okay...

CHORUS   It's dishonest.

MARK   I'm not proud. But seriously, some of those other applicants? Honey, you can't tell me that an engineer with a black belt in karate couldn't find a better job than in a furniture store. Dave needed my help.

CHORUS   He's a lifeguard.

MARK   Winter was setting in.

CHORUS   Wilson!

The CHORUS *form the furniture store.* MARK *talks to a cloaked and silent Mr. Wagner.*

MARK   They're gone, sir. I don't know; they were there last night.

CHORUS   The lifeguard.

MARK   You still have the lifeguard, sir. Now see, I just feel sick about this, sir.

CHORUS   The resumé.

MARK   The resumé I left with you yesterday. But sir, this is just awful.

CHORUS   David Sparkes.

MARK   Very nice guy, sir. I went and lost your stack of resumés. Your other options.

CHORUS   David.

MARK   Oh very, sir. Very nice guy. Who's kidding who? I hold myself totally responsible. I lost your stack of resumés and he's your only option.

CHORUS   Dave.

MARK   Very personable.

CHORUS   Yes.

MARK   So you'll take him?

CHORUS   What?

MARK   What?

CHORUS Terminated?

MARK But sir.

CHORUS Canned?

MARK But you wanted an extra on the floor?

CHORUS Fired.

MARK Let me explain... please!

CHORUS Goodbye, Wilson!

MARK Goodbye, Dave.

CHORUS Unemployed and in love.

The CHORUS *slowly retreat.* MARK *is alone.*

MARK   I wanted to work with him.

CHORUS   Work with him.

MARK   Okay, it was a stupid idea, but in no way was I asking to be fired. I just wanted to work with him. I admit it.

CHORUS   Work with him.

MARK   Someone my own age for once. Someone to talk to. A few things in common, even if they were all wingback and floral print. We could do lunch. Like, every day. Wear matching shirts. Share... trade secrets.

CHORUS   Carpool.

MARK   I had the opportunity to get to know this guy, harmless and healthy and hetero and...

CHORUS   I blow it.

MARK   I didn't even know if I'd even see him again.

DAVID   Hey... ah... I'm sorry.

Lights blare, illuminating the CHORUS *from behind in full choir formation.*

CHORUS   Hallelujah!

MARK   Mark.

CHORUS   Hallelujah!

DAVID   Mark, yeah. Got the call last night.

MARK   A mere twenty-three and three-quarter hours later I see him.

CHORUS Fate.

DAVID   Thanks a lot.

MARK   Oh don't thank me. I didn't really do anything.

DAVID   I guess.

MARK   When do you start?

DAVID   Tomorrow. Exciting huh?

MARK   That confusing urge to kiss and punch someone at the exact same time.

DAVID   Wagner seems nice.

MARK   Stay on his good side.

DAVID   Like you. Hey, will you, like, show me the ropes? I've never really done this kinda thing before.

MARK   God I had dreamt about him saying that.

DAVID   Not really up my alley, you know what I mean?

MARK   Sorry. I'm not working there any more.

DAVID   What?

MARK   I just decided that the job wasn't really right for me. Been doing a lot of thinking lately.

DAVID   Since yesterday?

MARK   It's been building, you know.

DAVID   Yeah, whatever. Listen, man, I gotta run. Nice talking to you.

MARK   Nice talking to you too.

CHORUS Don't stop talking.

MARK   I'll probably see you.

CHORUS Please don't stop talking.

MARK   You know, around.

CHORUS I'll give you a year to stop talking.

DAVID   Yeah, sure.

MARK   Goodbye.

CHORUS I love you.

DAVID   Goodbye.

CHORUS Have a nice day.

>   *The* CHORUS *slowly break out of choir formation as the backlighting fades.*

MARK   I am a bad gay man.

CHORUS   Bad gay man.

MARK   I mean technically I wasn't a "gay man." I was doing everything in my power not to be.

CHORUS   Bad gay man.

MARK   A sensible gay man would have made him breakfast by then, discussed the colour of his bed sheets while being tangled up in them. Me?

CHORUS   Bad gay man.

MARK   I didn't even know if he was gay. I didn't even know if I was.

CHORUS   Bad gay man.

MARK   I had decided, you see, somewhere around age fourteen, when junior high was a major low and the only thing more scary than Canada's National Fitness Test was the locker-room strip that immediately followed—I had decided that I would be... celibate. I knew that I could do this. Hey, my mom gave up gluten. So, you know, there's a testament to the enduring human spirit, or whatever. I figured, as long as no one knew, and as long as no one saw, and as long I could just... I could live my life as a reasonably happy "straight man." Whatevs, it just meant giving up all hope of true human connection. The same way Mom gave up dinner rolls.

CHORUS   Bad gay man.

MARK   And then ten years later, and there I was. And there he was. And… I'd only talked to this guy twice.

CHORUS   Twice about a furniture store.

MARK   And it had gone straight to my stomach. I couldn't eat. I couldn't sleep. I was a twelve-year-old girl and he was a poster on my wall.

CHORUS   Bad gay man.

MARK   I knew I could do this. And yet, there—in there—was this picture, at the back of my head. You know? Ever since I was that kid in gym class I had this image… this picture of…

CHORUS   The one for me.

MARK   Buried down deep, right. I'm talking sunk like the *Titanic* and yet still…

CHORUS   It's him.

MARK   In the flesh. Like a slap of cold water. Like somebody suddenly dug up this image from the bottom of me and made it real.

CHORUS   Made it breathe.

MARK   I had to see him again.

CHORUS   Think fast.

The CHORUS form a furniture store, with plenty of beds.

DAVID   A bed?

MARK   Yeah, a bed. You have them.

DAVID   Of course we have them. You know we have them.

MARK   Well?

DAVID   I just never thought a guy like you would shop in a store like this.

CHORUS   A guy like me?

DAVID   You would think after working here so long you would be sick of this shit.

MARK   You could say I've grown to love this place.

DAVID   You're frightening me. All we ever get in this place are People of Walmart. Polyester.

MARK   Twenty-five kids apiece.

DAVID   Yeah. Queen?

CHORUS   What?!

MARK   Excuse me.

DAVID   Queen size? Or are you going to go with the king?

MARK   No. No, queen size will be fine.

DAVID   I'll see what we have.

CHORUS   Talk to him.

MARK   So... how's it going?

DAVID   The job?

MARK   What else.

DAVID   It's a job, you know. Not really my cup of tea, but it's okay.

CHORUS   Ask him.

MARK   What is your cup of tea?

DAVID   The pool. Outdoors. Water, sunshine. As little clothing as possible.

MARK   That must be nice.

CHORUS   Ask him.

DAVID   It's great. But two months a year of work just don't cut it, you know what I mean?

CHORUS   Ask him.

MARK   Would you... like to go for a... grab a—a coffee, or something?

DAVID   A coffee?

MARK   Yeah. I mean you were saying you'd like some pointers on the job... you know, furniture. And I thought since it was so close to lunch we could go... you know... chat.

DAVID   Chat?

MARK   I can't believe I said chat.

MARK &
CHORUS   I cannot believe I said chat.

DAVID   Sure.

MARK   Yes?

DAVID   What do you think of this?

CHORUS   Our first date.

MARK   I think this is just great.

DAVID   Really?

CHORUS   He's talking about the bed.

MARK   Not really my style.

DAVID   Didn't think so.

CHORUS   New bed.

> MARK *wanders downstage centre as* DAVID *continues to search through the* CHORUS-*made selection of beds.*

MARK   I bought a bed for this man. I went into a furniture store and purchased an ugly bed just so I could see this man. I must've been completely insane.

CHORUS   New bed.

MARK   I had a bed. A perfectly good bed. I was unemployed and I went into the store from which I was aggressively fired just one week before and bought a butt-ugly bed I didn't even need just to see this man. I am totally insane.

CHORUS   Bonkers.

MARK   Cracked.

CHORUS   Stupid as hell.

MARK   But hey...

CHORUS   Stupid as hell.

MARK   ...we went for coffee.

The CHORUS *form a coffee counter.*

DAVID   That's crazy!

MARK   It's true, I swear.

DAVID   And he blamed you for it?

MARK   Took it out of my pay.

DAVID   Cream?

MARK   Black.

DAVID   That must have hurt.

MARK   Are you kidding? It hurt like hell. I mean that was like my second week of work. I was taking home three sixty-five after taxes. That was a good three weeks of work.

DAVID   Bet it never happened again.

MARK   No. After that whenever they walked through the door I politely asked them to spit out their gum, you know, finish their ice cream before they played on the merchandise.

DAVID   Point taken.

MARK   One of the most important lessons I've learned in retail. Never trust the customer. You end up with one stained couch and a lot less groceries.

DAVID   Any other secrets?

MARK   Thousands. You?

DAVID   Me?

CHORUS   You.

MARK   Yeah, you must have learned something about human nature working as a lifeguard.

DAVID   A little.

MARK   Well?

DAVID   Well, I learned to tell the difference between a person who is drowning and a person who is just farting around in the water.

MARK   Not much use away from the pool.

DAVID   I don't know. You learn to watch people. See their intentions. It's in their eyes, you know.

CHORUS   Watch people.

MARK   Yeah?

DAVID   Oh yeah. I got really good at telling whether someone was panicking or having the time of their life, just by looking in their eyes. I can spot panic a mile away. All in the eyes.

CHORUS   Panic.

MARK   Now that's talent.

DAVID   I'm serious. You can tell a lot about what a person is feeling just by looking in their eyes.

CHORUS   Their eyes!

MARK   Good coffee. You like this?

DAVID   Not a big coffee drinker, but yeah, yeah it's nice.

MARK   Ever been to Pablo's?

DAVID   Friend of yours?

MARK   A place in the square. A mean cup. It could convert you.

DAVID   I don't know. I'm a tea man myself.

MARK   So was I.

DAVID   Ah, but Pablo's.

MARK   Yes indeed.

DAVID   You awakened.

MARK   Found myself.

DAVID   Came out of the closet as the true coffee lover you had always been.

MARK   Well...

CHORUS Closet.

MARK   ...I mean...

CHORUS Lover.

MARK   ...it was just around the corner from work.

DAVID   Work! Shit, what time is it?

MARK   You have five minutes.

DAVID   Sorry, gotta run.

MARK   Sure.

CHORUS Don't go.

DAVID   Listen, thanks for the pointers.

MARK   Um, sure. Yeah.

CHORUS   Don't let him go.

DAVID   I'll probably see you around.

MARK   Yeah.

CHORUS   You can't let him go!

DAVID   Bye.

MARK   Later.

CHORUS   Stop him!

MARK   Listen, Dave…

DAVID   Yeah?

MARK   I am going to be… coincidentally enough… up around there on Wednesday. The square? For some completely random reason that I can't lay my mind to right now…

CHORUS   Shut up!

MARK   Anyway, I'll be around. Wednesday. You know, if you want to check out Pablo's. I mean—

DAVID   Wednesday?

MARK   Best coffee in town. It'll really change your life.

DAVID   I'm going to hold you to that. See you Wednesday.

CHORUS   Hold me.

MARK   Yeah. Bye.

CHORUS   Love you.

DAVID   Bye.

CHORUS   Bye.

> The CHORUS *dissolve the coffee counter and form a low chat circle on the floor.* MARK *turns to us.*

MARK   Sooooo...

CHORUS   What do you want?

MARK   I don't know. Part of me just wanted to get to know him better. Okay? Okay, part of me just wanted to get to know him. So I could hopefully, possibly see that this, all of this, was nothing. Was... normal. Just a... just a bromance, really, just a bromance, man—nothing more than the flickering beginnings of a potentially beautiful friendship, a friendship that would one day see us, I don't know, being each other's wing man, or each other's best man, or, you know... taking out the hogs for a spin. Just... just a normal, everyday, very... *masculine* friendship that would see me eventually perfectly happy and content with it all and soooooo not wanting to fall into his eyes or get into his pants, because, hey, that's just Dave, Davie, my buddy Daverino, my bro, my homes, my homeslice.

CHORUS   What do you want?

MARK   Part of me wanted that.

CHORUS   What do you want?

MARK   And part of me didn't. Part of me was being pulled— pulled along by all of this, and him, and all the other stupid undeniable parts of me, pulled against my will and my cowardice into something all together new and scary and pointless, and... unbelievable. And...

CHORUS   Beautiful.

MARK   Part of me was really... falling in love.

CHORUS   The proof.

> MARK *rises and begins to walk downstage centre. The* CHORUS *rise and form a large high-walled box of sheets, with themselves inside.*

MARK   Walking home from coffee that day, for the first time in my life I was struck by the incredible beauty of every person, place, and thing I passed.

The CHORUS *in their sheet box are backlit to reveal shadows of paired dancers. They begin to sing "Für Elise."* MARK *dances dreamily and deliriously with a solo* CHORUS *shadow front and centre.*

I love him!

MARK *collapses into the arms of four* CHORUS *members, who then form his new bed.* MARK *is drowsy, on the edge of sleep.*

CHORUS New bed.

MARK   My new bed he sold me. Ugly as hell, but if you closed your eyes and used your imagination it kinda smelled like him. A bit too firm for my taste, but I wasn't complaining.

DAVID *enters* MARK*'s bedroom. The lighting and sound are eerie. Something is not right.*

DAVID   Nice place you got.

MARK   It's all right.

DAVID   Doesn't even have a door.

MARK   My dad. He thought I should be able to leave now and then.

DAVID   And do you?

MARK   No. Not yet.

DAVID   So you're a hermit. You're missing all the action. You want some pizza?

MARK   No thanks, I'm not thirsty. Can we talk?

DAVID   This is really dangerous, Mark. No door. People can come right in. You should get a door.

MARK   I have to tell you something, Dave.

DAVID   Call me David.

MARK   Do I have to?

DAVID   Yes.

MARK   David—

DAVID   I know exactly what you are going to say.

MARK   All right.

DAVID   You don't really want to kiss me, do you?

MARK   I think so.

DAVID   If I kiss you I'll dry up into nothing. You know that.

MARK   Yeah.

DAVID   Hey, there's a parade outside. They're setting fire to the houses across the street. You should come.

MARK   I have asthma. Thanks though.

DAVID   That's what friends are for. They're calling my name. I have to go.

MARK   I feel younger.

DAVID   We all feel younger, Mark. That just means you're growing up.

> DAVID *exits, moving stage left to a huddled group of the* CHORUS. *After he is gone:*

MARK   I don't care. I don't care if you dry up into dust. I don't. At least then I'll know exactly what you are.

CHORUS   Close your eyes.

> DAVID *speaks to the huddled group of* CHORUS. *They laugh loudly.*

DAVID   Ever hear the one about the gay magician? He vanished with a poof. No listen, okay, listen, how do you fit three fags on one bar stool? You just turn it upside down.

No seriously, listen, how many fags does it take to screw in a light bulb? One, but it takes an entire emergency room to remove it. Oh, yeah I know, yeah I know, boo-hoo awful right? Yeah well you try having him in your business all the time, all doughy-eyed and full of morning pride. You see his face, man? Take a good look. Look at him! He hates himself more than I ever could.

CHORUS   No!

MARK *wakes up in his new bed with a start. Silence.*

Don't be the joke.

Wednesday.

The CHORUS *form Pablo's coffee shop.*

DAVID   What?

MARK   It was just a question.

DAVID   I don't know. I don't get out very much these days.

MARK   You don't like coffee. You don't go out.

CHORUS   A mystery.

DAVID   Correction, I didn't like coffee. You were right. This place has changed my life.

MARK   So, what kind of music you into?

DAVID   Jeez, curious much?

CHORUS   I love you.

MARK   I love music. I was just wondering if you did... too.

DAVID   Yeah, sure, I like music.

MARK   What kind?

DAVID   Are you writing a book or something?

CHORUS   Dear diary.

MARK   No, I just—

DAVID   Well what about you?

MARK   What about me?

DAVID   What are you into?

CHORUS   What are *you* into?

DAVID   Mark?

MARK   Sorry, could you repeat the question?

DAVID   You love music so much. Do you go out?

MARK   Well, I'm not a hermit, I—

DAVID   No, I mean where do you go, where do you hang out?

MARK   Does the EI office count?

DAVID   There's just this DJ.

MARK   Oh? Okay.

DAVID   He's called Slim Macho. Local guy. Really...

CHORUS   Fruity!

DAVID   ...fierce.

MARK   Never heard of him.

DAVID   Well he's on tonight, and I haven't seen him in a while,
         so. Thinking I might head down; if you want you can—

MARK   Sure. Where?

DAVID   He's spinning at Club Foot.

MARK   Oh.

CHORUS   Club Foot.

MARK   Okay.

CHORUS   Club Foot.

DAVID   Mark?

MARK   Yeah. What?

DAVID   You up for it?

CHORUS   Club Foot.

MARK   Sure. I mean, yes. Yeah. Totally.

DAVID   How about we meet here at around nine.

MARK   Sounds... good. To me.

DAVID   I gotta run.

MARK   Yeah, bye.

CHORUS   Nine o'clock p.m.

DAVID   Later.

CHORUS   Club Foot.

The CHORUS *dissolve Pablo's.* MARK *steps downstage centre into a spotlight that already contains* DAVID.

MARK   He invited me to Club Foot.

CHORUS   Club Foot.

MARK   The city's finest, largest, best-known GAY BAR. In point of fact, it was the city's only gay bar. Nevertheless! A gay bar! And this one? Only mythic, legendary, infamous. A reputation to make your mother faint, and then pick herself up and put on some heels and a tube top. A party in a box and so much more.

CHORUS   In short.

MARK   There was no way you could live in this city more than five minutes without knowing what was behind those big pink doors.

CHORUS   Club Foot.

The CHORUS *form Club Foot. Dancers hold coloured flashlights that rhythmically pulse to the* CHORUS-*created dance music.* MARK *looks uncomfortable.*

MARK   Wow, is it always this crazy?

DAVID   I don't know. Good crowd, though, eh?

MARK   I don't know what I was so afraid of. Setting off some nelly detector when I walked in the door?

DAVID   You want a beer?

MARK   Yeah, sure. Okay, so he takes me to Club Foot. Terrifying, yes, but I went. If there was ever a chance to find out what side of the fence this guy pitched his tent…

CHORUS   This would be it.

MARK   Most straight guys would never be caught dead going in there.

DAVID   He's good, eh?

MARK   Yeah? How come I haven't heard of him before?

DAVID   Plays here all the time.

MARK   Really?

DAVID   Have you ever been here before?

MARK   No. You?

DAVID   Nah. But I've always been curious.

CHORUS   Curious.

MARK   Curious?

DAVID   Well, you know, big pink doors. People are always talking about this place.

MARK   What do they say?

DAVID   Best dance club in the city. Friends of mine swear by it.

CHORUS   Friends.

DAVID   What?

MARK   Nothing.

DAVID   He's really great, eh?

MARK   Okay, it was crazy. Going there, to Club Foot, with him. In hindsight I get that, okay. It was like seeing if the water is boiling by throwing yourself into it. It was dumb and foolish and, and unnecessary, really, when all I needed to do was ask him. Just look him in the eye and ask him.

Just ask him, that's all. Just ask him. Just ask him. Ask him. Ask him. Ask him.

MARK &
CHORUS Just ask him!

MARK Dave!

The CHORUS *form a semicircle around* MARK *and* DAVID, *focusing their flashlights in on them. The music shifts to a soft lullaby.*

And there it was... the look. That was the first time I'd seen it. He stood there in this crowd. People pushing. And he was so... serene. Perfect.

DAVID Perfect?

MARK As close as I'd ever seen.

DAVID Aw, thanks.

MARK You stood there with that stupid smile on your face, looking so... there.

DAVID I was there.

MARK No, I mean... connected. Like... like everything depended on my next word.

DAVID Maybe everything did, Mark.

A pause as they stare at each other.

Mark? Hello. You okay? You were like a million miles away.

MARK   You... you want to take off?

DAVID   What? No, no, man, I'm liking this.

MARK   I'm thinking I might head out.

DAVID   Okay, cool. See you later, man.

> MARK *slowly backs away as* DAVID *goes back to watching the DJ.*

MARK   And just like that, we went from potential, to actual, right back to potential. In the space of five seconds.

DAVID   This guy is just fierce!

> MARK *turns and leaves. The* CHORUS *begin to separate. The music picks up tempo.*

MARK   And I left. I had no choice. I left him to get away from him, to go home and sleep on a bed that reminded me of him.

CHORUS Goodbye.

MARK   Do we hunt out memories or do they hunt out us?

DAVID   Mark!

CHORUS Pablo's!

The CHORUS *form Pablo's.*

DAVID   Changed my life.

CHORUS   My table.

MARK   He was sitting at my table. This was getting too weird.

DAVID   You were right, you know.

MARK   I was?

DAVID   The coffee.

MARK   Stick with me, kid.

DAVID   Got a minute?

MARK   Ah... sure... yeah sure.

DAVID   Coffee?

MARK   No... I'm trying to cut down.

DAVID   So you get me hooked? Fourth cup.

MARK   You're kidding.

DAVID   Can't live without the stuff.

CHORUS   Must be rough.

DAVID   What happened to you the other night? You should have stuck around.

MARK   I was tired, you know.

DAVID   You missed his best set, man.

MARK   Yeah?

DAVID   Yeah. Oh, and hey, I met your mom!

MARK &
CHORUS What?!

MARK   My mom, you...?

DAVID   Yeah.

MARK   At the club?

DAVID   No, dingus. She came in the store the other day, when I was—

MARK   The store. Shit.

DAVID   Yeah, looking for you, actually. Seemed to think you'd be there.

MARK   Yeah I might have neglected to tell her that I... you know.

DAVID   You didn't tell your mom that you changed jobs?

MARK   Changed jobs. That would have been an excellent way to put it. You met her?

DAVID   Yeah. She's... friendly.

CHORUS   Friendly.

MARK   My mother? Was friendly?

DAVID   Sure. Really friendly; we talked about furniture.

MARK   Is that all?

DAVID   And appliances. Top load versus front load, you know.

MARK   The eternal debate. Hope it didn't get too heated.

DAVID   Well, actually, I'm afraid I... well, I think I must've said something because she just...

MARK   She just what?

DAVID   She just went... sour.

CHORUS   Sour.

DAVID   Suddenly. Just took off like a flash.

MARK   She went sour?

DAVID   Yeah, I mean, I didn't mean to—

> MARK *rises to leave.*

MARK   It's fine, no worries.

CHORUS   Sour.

DAVID   I don't know what it was I said, I—

MARK   It's fine. Listen, I gotta go. Later

CHORUS   I love you.

> MARK *goes to leave but* DAVID *calls out after him.*

DAVID   She was really friendly though.

CHORUS   Mom.

> MARK *talks to his mother on the phone.*

MARK   What do you mean you don't remember? Sour. You went sour, Mom. Those were his exact words...

CHORUS   David.

MARK   His name is David, and no... no he didn't steal my job; I quit, if you must know... I don't know why that's so funny, Mom. I am quite capable of holding down a job if I...

CHORUS   David.

MARK   His name is David... Well, yeah, yeah I know, Mom, but some people see the inherent benefits of the front-loading washer, the water savings, and the... What?

CHORUS   Fag.

MARK   He's not a homosexual, Mom, why would you...

CHORUS   Fag.

MARK   He's not a… you always think that… just because a man compliments your blouse instead of your boobs, you go off thinking they're gay. I mean, Jesus, you…

MARK &
CHORUS   No. No.

MARK   I don't care if he is or if he isn't and, and neither should you, really, I mean …

CHORUS   Ho. Mo.

MARK   He…? Asking about me? What do you mean asking about…? That doesn't make him a homo, Mom.

MARK &
CHORUS   No. No.

MARK   Because! He… He said what? He…?

CHORUS   Oh. Oh.

MARK   Oh.

Oh…

Okay…

Goodbye, Mom.

MARK hangs up. He is stupefied.

Any woman would be lucky to have me.

CHORUS   Any woman would be lucky to have me.

MARK   That's what he said. That's what he told MY MOM.

CHORUS   Any woman would be lucky to have me.

MARK   That was the nicest thing anyone had ever said about me. My confused, delighted little lump of a heart slopping like a bucket too full because a beautiful stupid person liked me.

CHORUS   He doesn't know.

MARK   And thought that I might be normal enough to be into chicks.

CHORUS   Happy?

MARK   Sure. Yeah. I was happy; I admit it. In that way that's dangerous. That negates rational decision-making.

CHORUS   Happy.

MARK   This, this here required some... restraint. Some alone time. Some deep personal reflection.

CHORUS   Yes.

MARK *is in a yoga class.*

MARK   Yeah, well I've been sleeping like an angel on this new bed. Pillow top, so worth the money. Yeah, I'll totally hook you up. My buddy Dave works there now.

CHORUS   David Sparkes.

MARK   Oh, my buddy David? You know him? Yeah, we're pretty tight.

In a coffee shop.

I used to take my coffee black but my friend Dave, he does this combo thing with milk AND cream that's honestly to die for. It's, like, really... creative. Yeah, he's great.

CHORUS   David Sparkes.

MARK   Yeah, look him up, and add him. Sparkes, that's S P A R...

At the club, dancing, watching the DJ.

I know, right?! He's totally fierce! My buddy David introduced me to him. You know him? David?

CHORUS   David Sparkes.

In a store, trying on a shirt that's too tight.

MARK   My friend. Yeah, well I'm thinking of taking up swimming. Because David says it's like really good for your upper body, and well he... he's a lifeguard, so. He's like totally... fit, or whatever.

CHORUS   David Sparkes.

MARK   Yeah.

Yeah, we're pretty tight.

Night at a campground in the woods. MARK *is very drunk. He screams into the night.*

He is my best friend! The best friend that, like, I ever had. So. Yeah! To David.

He toasts grandly and drinks.

And fuck you, Mom.

FUUUUUUUUCCCCCCKKKK! YOOOOOUUUUUU!

A change in place and light.

CHORUS   Today.

MARK begins to move to centre stage.

MARK   So.

CHORUS   So?

MARK   So I knew I was totally lovable, right? Right? I mean, I was worthy of love—regardless of what else I might have been, I was worthy of that. I mean check out these cheeks. A sense of humour, caring and considerate and smart. Totally smart, right? I mean, clearly!

CHORUS   So?

MARK   And so, you know, I was just gonna be me. Because me, I am pretty fantastic. Right? The me I am, the me I was was pretty... was good enough, right? Regardless. So... so I decided. I decided... fuck celibacy. I decided that I was just going to be the me that I was born to be, and I was going to... I was going to tell Dave. Without hope or agenda, I was going to tell him, tell Mr. David Sparkes that Mark Wilson is a... an openly... an out, and... a, you know, gay... a gay homosexual... man.

CHORUS   Hallelujah!

MARK   And then I was gonna tell him I love him and he was gonna say, well that's retarded, and I was gonna say, well first of all, Dave, retarded is a really offensive word. And then he was gonna say that he was a gay homosexual too.

        Silence.

CHORUS   And?

MARK   Then he'd tell me that he loves me, that he wanted to spend the rest of his life with me. Tell me how his life too had been a vacuous collection of wasted years waiting at the precipice of despair, just waiting for me to show up and rescue him and to usher him into a perfectly normal and golden future including a new lakeside home and a beachfront wedding and a four-day workweek and Asian adoption and southern vacations and organic gardening and early retirement and grandkids at Christmas.

CHORUS   And?

MARK   I didn't expect him to have the engagement ring on him. I mean, I was willing to wait.

CHORUS   Days, weeks, months, years.

MARK   And that was okay. I wasn't being unreasonable.

          The CHORUS *form Pablo's.* MARK *and* DAVID *are in line at the counter.*

DAVID   God does love unconditionally, but there are certain provisos.

MARK   Pentecostal.

DAVID   And see, that makes sense. A lot of what he said made sense.

CHORUS   Pentecostal.

DAVID   His sermon was great, so after the service I caught up with him. Great guy, really liberal.

MARK   He's Pentecostal.

DAVID   And I mean I think that's what the clergy needs today.

CHORUS   A practising Pentecostal.

DAVID   Ministers who understand the young people. Who want to bond with them.

CHORUS   I fell in love with a practising Pentecostal.

DAVID   Mark?

MARK   Huh? Yeah?

DAVID   You okay?

MARK   Yeah, yeah sure.

DAVID   You've hardly touched your coffee.

MARK   Yeah, I've just reached my limit.

DAVID   May I?

> MARK *nods.* DAVID *turns and walks away speaking. The* CHORUS *form a large backlit crucifix that* MARK *stares at intently during the following.*

So he was talking about sin, and sinners specifically, and how all sinners are loved by God, but how they can only benefit from that love if they return this... this love that God gives. So, as he was saying, God's love is unconditional in that he can forgive sin and love the sinner, but only provided that the sinner love God in return. Now see, I think that's fair. I mean really it is.

How unfair of us to expect God to just be on call and for us never to put any effort in. You think about what an incredible task it must be to love the entire universe. I mean, what... there's like six... seven billion people in the world. Seven billion people. Imagine having to love seven billion people. Listen to their prayers, care about what they're saying. Seven billion people... and that's only assuming that there's no life on other planets. Loving seven billion people that don't love you back... I mean, fuck... right? So it's not unreasonable to expect that even the maker of heaven and earth needs to be loved. Needs a hug now and then. What do you think?

MARK   Do you think I'm fat?

DAVID   What?

MARK   Do you think I'm fat?

CHORUS   Ugly.

DAVID   No.

MARK   Do you think I'm attractive?

DAVID   I don't see what this has to do with sin.

CHORUS   Fugly.

    The CHORUS *dissolve the crucifix.*

MARK   I feel ugly. I mean, I always have, you know. But there are some days, and, boy, this is one of them.

DAVID   Are you okay?

MARK   Do you go to church a lot?

DAVID   A lot?

MARK   Once a week? Once a month? Or is it like Christmas, Easter, and weddings?

DAVID   Usually once a week or so.

CHORUS   Once a week.

MARK   I see.

DAVID   Well, I mean now. Not always. Just the last month or so. I've just needed it, you know.

MARK   Your family Pentecostal?

DAVID   Is this important?

CHORUS   Yes.

MARK   No, just curious.

DAVID   Not practising, no.

CHORUS   Not practising.

DAVID   Are you sure you're okay?

CHORUS   No.

MARK   Yes. I just need to get some sleep.

DAVID   You're going?

MARK   Yeah, listen, thanks a lot for coffee and… and I guess I will see you later.

DAVID   I guess.

MARK   Bye.

CHORUS   Pentecostal.

DAVID   Bye.

CHORUS   Bless you.

> The CHORUS *form a church, complete with altar, minister, and singing congregation.*

MARK   Was I overreacting?

CHORUS   Yes.

MARK   I've been known to do that.

CHORUS   Yes.

MARK   I'd known him for over a month. You think that would have come up.

CHORUS   Pentecostal.

MARK   Jesus.

CHORUS   Yes.

MARK   Well I clearly didn't know him as well as I thought, right?

CHORUS   Pentecostal.

MARK   So I had… I have… this paranoid fear of Pentecostals. Just as well to say.

CHORUS   Practising Pentecostals.

MARK   Not all Pentecostals. Just the ones who… practise. But so what, right? What's the big deal? He'd just committed his life to an ethical code that would see me roasted on a spit for eternity; I mean, that didn't mean we couldn't hang out. Right?

CHORUS   Yes.

MARK Right?

CHORUS Yes!

MARK Well I can't blame this on my parents or faulty genetics. This is all your fault.

CHORUS No.

MARK No, no it's not.

CHORUS Practising Pentecostal.

MARK It's not your fault. Not even close. Just another one of mine. Yet another fault of mine. One more fucking fault that I stick to myself, that I can call my own—my fault not yours, you perfect beautiful thing you—just one more thing I can add to the list of stuff that you hate; I'll add it and I'll be it, I swear to God I'll be all of it; I'll find myself in it, I'll define myself by it, I'll be nothing but it, and I'll find myself drowning in it—I'll be drowning and I'll say okay, okay, okay, it's okay to drown, it's totally okay to finally FINALLY whither and die and cease to exist because I probably shouldn't have anyway. I probably should never have even been…!

A silent pause. MARK *has upset himself. This is not funny anymore. He slowly recovers.*

(*quietly*) I don't want to do this. I don't want to remember anymore.

CHORUS Fag.

The CHORUS *dissolve the church.* DAVID *appears. Loud* CHORUS *laughter.*

DAVID How do you know? No, listen, listen, how do you know when you've walked into a fag-friendly church, eh? Eh? Well, for starters, only half the congregation is kneeling.

The laughter ceases. MARK *wakes in bed alone.*

MARK Jesus.

Fuck.

Fuck.

He groans in frustration.

I need some sleep. I need some...

CHORUS Courage.

A montage of scenes. DAVID *attempts to find and talk to* MARK. MARK *uses the various* CHORUS *formations to hide behind.*

DAVID Hey, Mark...! Mark... Mark, buddy... Hey, Mark, it's me... Mark...! Mark, give me a call when you get in... Hey, Mark...! Mark! Over here... Mark!

CHORUS Mark.

DAVID Mark.

CHORUS Mark.

DAVID   Mark.

CHORUS   Mark.

DAVID &

CHORUS   It's me...

CHORUS   ...David.

DAVID   ...David.

CHORUS   Don't you remember me?

DAVID   David.

CHORUS   David Sparkes.

DAVID   The man you love.

CHORUS   The man you are in love with.

DAVID   The straight man that you are in love with.

CHORUS   The man that doesn't know.

DAVID   Tell me, Mark. Tell me you're gay. Tell me you love me. I'm the man of your dreams. Tell me, Mark. Tell me, Mark.

DAVID &

CHORUS   Tell me!

MARK   I need some time!

CHORUS   I needed some time.

The CHORUS *form Pablo's.*

DAVID   Hey, stranger, where have you been?

MARK   Busy.

DAVID   Busy?

CHORUS   Busy.

DAVID   How was your week?

MARK   Good.

DAVID   Good... listen, can we talk?

CHORUS   No.

DAVID   Mark?

MARK   Yeah. Yeah, I need to talk to you too.

DAVID   Me first, okay?

CHORUS   No.

MARK   David, please—

DAVID   Mark, this is important.

CHORUS   No.

MARK   I've been thinking a lot, Dave, and I—

DAVID   Mark, I'm—

MARK   I've been thinking, and I—

DAVID   Please, just—

CHORUS No.

MARK   And I need to tell you something.

DAVID   Mark, just let me—

MARK   Something important—

DAVID   Mark, please—

CHORUS No.

DAVID   *(to CHORUS)* Shut up! Just shut up!

> MARK *is stunned.*

Look, this is important.

MARK   Yeah, well this is pretty important too.

DAVID   Mark—

MARK   I've put this off too long, Dave. And I need you to know.
        I need you to know that—

DAVID *steps in close and clasps his hand over* MARK's
*mouth, shutting him up. It is a silent and undefined
moment, a moment that could slide any way and* MARK
is unsure of what is happening.

DAVID   *(quietly)* Mark. I'm... I'm going to be a father.

There is a pause as MARK *attempts to catch his breath.
He fails and faints into the arms of the* CHORUS.
Lights out.

Act 2

Spotlight on MARK *alone.*

CHORUS   How are you?

MARK   Fine.

CHORUS   How are you?

MARK   I'm fine.

CHORUS   How are you?

MARK   Fine. I'm fine.

CHORUS   How are you?

MARK   I said I'm fine!

CHORUS   How are you?

MARK   Fine, all right! I'm fucking fine. I'm great. Peachy. Perfect. He's straight. She's pregnant. Why the hell wouldn't I be fine. I'm just great. I'm fine.

The CHORUS *form Pablo's.* DAVID *enters.*

DAVID   You sure?

MARK slowly sits at the table with DAVID.

MARK   Yeah. Yeah. Don't know what happened there. Got a little light-headed. I haven't been feeling well.

DAVID   Join the club.

MARK   How are you?

DAVID   Tired. Confused. Terrified.

MARK   How long?

DAVID   A month? I don't know.

MARK   Who... who is she?

DAVID   My girlfriend... my ex. My wife, I don't know.

MARK   Marriage?

DAVID   I don't think that's my decision anymore.

MARK   You don't have to.

CHORUS   Pentecostal.

MARK   Do you want to? Get married, I mean?

DAVID   I don't know what I want, Mark.

MARK A baby. Wow.

DAVID Jesus, just hearing it makes me... Ah, fuck, I'm pretty sure I don't want that.

MARK What does she want?

DAVID She's thinking. Just needed some time she said.

MARK She could... there are options.

DAVID I know.

MARK Ones you don't like.

DAVID I didn't say that.

MARK Oh. Okay.

  Beat.

  It's going to be all right.

DAVID Yeah.

MARK It is. Look at me.

  David.

  It's going to be all right.

  Okay?

CHORUS Why?

The CHORUS *dissolve Pablo's.* MARK *moves to centre stage.*

MARK Because it had to be. Because he deserved it to be.

I remember my father once said that you don't know a person until you know them in sadness.

This was the moment that I met you. The full of you.

Beat.

And this was the moment that you asked for friendship. And the moment that I said okay. Because I thought I could handle it.

CHORUS No such luck.

The CHORUS *form* MARK's *living room.*

DAVID I'm thinking about the guitar.

MARK Really?

DAVID Yeah. Yeah, I need a hobby. I mean everyone has a hobby, right. You write.

MARK Try to write.

DAVID I need something like that.

MARK A hobby.

DAVID Yeah, for six months now my life has been furniture, furniture, and more furniture. I need a hobby.

MARK   So buy one.

DAVID   I did. Second-hand. Really nice.

MARK   Lessons?

DAVID   Going to teach myself.

MARK   Ambitious.

DAVID   You sing, right?

MARK   What?

DAVID   You sing. I heard you. At Nicole's the other night.

MARK   I was drunk.

DAVID   Tell me about it.

MARK   Well, I wasn't that drunk.

DAVID   You really really were.

MARK   What are you, my mother?

DAVID   Look, point being, you can sing, Mark.

MARK   So?

DAVID   So, we should do something together.

CHORUS   Yes we should!

DAVID   I'll learn the guitar, and we can form a band. You sing.

MARK   Just like that?

DAVID   I need a hobby, Mark.

MARK   I tell you what—if you really learn to play that guitar, I'll learn to sing.

DAVID   And we'll start a band?

MARK   Legends in the making.

CHORUS   Legends.

The CHORUS dissolve MARK's living room.

MARK   Amazing, really, how much time two people can spend together and not talk about anything. Anything that matters. That winter we formed a band. Learned conversational French. Took up fly-tying. Photography lessons, judo lessons. Pottery lessons. Together, we brought denial and avoidance to new heights of stupidity.

CHORUS   Silent partner.

The CHORUS form a solid wall upstage centre and a card table centre stage.

DAVID   Okay, lows in black means twos are tens and tens are twos and vice versa all the way down, four three two up two three four in red. This progression grows until you get to the ace, unless of course it is a trump when

you skip the five and jack, which lead in red ten queen
king ace jack five—that's only true in hearts or in diamonds—it's ten queen king ace ace of hearts jack five
and in black two queen king ace ace of hearts jack five.
Some people play that ace is low in black, which means
there's only one high ace which is true and that is the ace
of diamonds. Clubs and spades are low and the ace of
hearts is wild and always third high no matter what the
suit. If you're finishing off a round of forty-fives however
and ace of spades and ace of clubs are head to head ace
of clubs wins because ace of spades is the lowest in the
deck, don't ask me why, there's no reason really, it's just
a rule.

MARK   What?

DAVID   So if I'm your partner… hmm… what's your pleasure?
Jack your partner?

MARK   What?

DAVID   Silent partner?

MARK   What?

DAVID   Great, I love silent partner too. So this is where your
partner doesn't know he is but you know he is as soon
as he lays his partner cards on the table. He never finds
out who he is until the end of the round 'cause say you
want the ace of hearts but the person with the ace of
hearts thinks you want the jack but you don't 'cause
you're looking for his heart, he might just assume you
don't want the heart and play against you, but what you
wanted all along was for him to lay into you but he never

knew so you both lose unless, which I have seen happen, he thinks he's not your partner and he reneges.

MARK What?

DAVID Holds back his heart and beats you on an easy one. You think you've lost but his heart comes out last minute. I don't allow reneging at my games, too easy to get burned.

MARK What?

CHORUS Burned.

> The CHORUS *dissolve the card table. They form a seat with a telephone.* MARK *is on the phone.*

MARK Yes, Mom, I've got some resumés out. I'll make some calls tomorrow. I'll...

CHORUS No.

MARK What do you want me to say then, Mom? Just tell me and I'll say it, I... I'm not.

CHORUS No.

MARK Well maybe you should have, Mom, maybe you shoulda had other kids, some less disappointing ones; I sure coulda used the hand-me-downs.

CHORUS No.

MARK I'm sorry. I'm sorry, I know... I know you only... yeah. Yes, I miss him too.

CHORUS   No.

MARK   I know. You're lonely. I imagine that must be very
          difficult.

          DAVID appears centre stage behind MARK.

DAVID   Did you hear about the two fags that got in a fight at
          the queer bar? Yeah, they had to go outside to exchange
          blows.

CHORUS   Don't be the joke.

          MARK *is still on the phone.*

MARK   No, I don't... I don't want you to worry about me.

CHORUS   Yes.

MARK   I am nothing... nothing, Mom, that you should be wor-
          ried about. Really.

          Really.

DAVID   Hey, Marco.

CHORUS   Marco?

          The CHORUS *form Pablo's.*

DAVID   Mark, listen, do you like camping?

MARK   You mean like sleeping bags, mosquitoes, bear shit
          camping?

DAVID   Yeah.

MARK   It has its moments.

DAVID   This weekend. Me and you. A men's retreat.

CHORUS   A men's retreat.

MARK   Open fire? Raw meat? Lean-to?

DAVID   My folks' cabin, actually. Roughing it for a few nights.

CHORUS   Roughing it.

DAVID   I figure we head out Friday night, stay until Sunday, and we get back in time for wing night. Just to get away for a while, you know.

MARK   Where?

DAVID   A forty-minute drive. You'll love it, come on.

MARK   I don't know.

DAVID   Come on.

MARK   I'm just not that great with nature. We don't get along.

DAVID   Don't get along?

MARK   Bad childhood experience.

DAVID   Don't worry, I'll take care of you.

MARK Take care of me?

DAVID Yeah.

CHORUS Take care of me.

The CHORUS *dissolve Pablo's.*

MARK Oh for God's sake just come out already. It's not like I didn't have the wardrobe. If I could reach through time and shake myself. A men's retreat?

DAVID re-enters. They are packing to leave.

DAVID Is that what you wanted? To be taken care of?

MARK looks at him. Beat. He forces a smile, jokes.

MARK Carried across a threshold. Every girl's dream.

DAVID It's good to see you smiling.

Beat.

MARK Don't. Don't say that.

DAVID Why not?

MARK Because I'm not. I'm not smiling, not really, and you, you're not seeing anything anymore. You're not even here.

And this can stop. All this, it can, any time I want.

DAVID You can't control the ending.

And besides, some of it was good.

MARK Some of it. Some of it was. What happened. Some of it...
is worth remembering. So sue me, some of it can still
make me smile.

DAVID You were happy.

MARK In a sick, twisted, asexual, keep-your-mind-on-other-
things sort of way, yeah.

Beat.

What choice did I have? But keep my mind on other
things? I'd gotten really good at it. I still am.

CHORUS Play it by ear.

MARK I could teach a class in it, you know. Being stupid.

DAVID And deaf.

MARK Dumb.

CHORUS Blind.

The lights go out. MARK *and* DAVID *are speaking in
the dark.*

DAVID Got it?

MARK Where?

DAVID Far wall on the left.

In the darkness MARK *trips—a bang.*

MARK   Shit!

DAVID   You okay?

MARK   It's dark.

DAVID   Be careful.

MARK   Over the woodpile?

DAVID   Yeah that's it.

> *Lights up. The* CHORUS *have formed the interior of* DAVID'*s cabin.*

MARK   What a stupid place to hang a lantern.

DAVID   Used to be a door over there. Closed it up a few years ago. In winter the wind used to whip right through her.

MARK   It's nice.

DAVID   Dad's pride and joy.

MARK   He built it?

DAVID   With my uncle. Mom and Dad used to spend every weekend out here. Don't get out much anymore.

MARK   Electric heat and everything. Nice.

DAVID   Yeah.

MARK   Bring the stuff in?

DAVID   It can wait.

MARK   You okay?

DAVID   Yeah. Yeah, fine.

MARK   It's cold in here. Can I turn on the heat?

DAVID   Sure.

MARK   Jesus, it's so odd to have electric heat up here. Seems so detached. Miles from the nearest house. You wouldn't think the power company would be so ready and willing to thread some lines up here. All the way up here just for some little cabin in the middle of nowhere.

DAVID   Generator.

MARK   Of course. I knew that. Where is it? You want me to fire it up? I hope you got some gas in here. I had no idea this place would have a generator. You said we were going to rough it.

DAVID   This weekend.

        It could have been, you know? It could have been this weekend.

        MARK looks at him, realizes what he is saying. A pause.

MARK   Yeah?

DAVID   Nine months last week.

MARK   I... I didn't know you were counting.

DAVID   Neither did I.

MARK   She did the right thing.

DAVID   Did she?

          Beat.

MARK   You're having regrets.

DAVID   Not regrets. Thoughts. Just lots and lots of thoughts.

MARK   Same thing.

DAVID   No. It's not. There is nothing in this world as frightening as regret.

MARK   I don't know about that.

DAVID   I do. I've spent my whole life avoiding it. This is not regret. It's something different.

MARK   Better?

DAVID   Different.

MARK   Better. If it's different it's better.

DAVID   I don't want to regret this, Mark.

I don't want to regret anything.

MARK You won't.

I promise.

Pause.

Do you keep your gas in here?

DAVID Yeah. Out in the back.

CHORUS Two days.

> *The* CHORUS *form the interior of* DAVID's *car.* MARK *sits in the passenger seat looking out the window while* DAVID *drives.*

MARK Two days in a cabin, alone with that man. It would have been less of a horror show if I'd gone insane and eaten his liver.

CHORUS   Two days.

MARK   Separate rooms, and I could still hear him breathing at
          night. The walls bending with it, his bed creaking from
          down the hall.

CHORUS   Insane.

MARK   Jesus, I thought I would, you know. I really thought I'd
          go insane. Before I went up I thought I would pull my
          hair out. Having to see him, talk to him for two whole
          days without any other human contact.

CHORUS   Temptation. Frustration.

MARK   Before that weekend everything was fine. It totally was,
          in retrospect. It was always fine. Better than fine.

CHORUS   Perfect.

MARK   I mean, sure, it always felt like the next time I'd see him
          I'd have an aneurism, but the next time I did see him it
          was... beautiful.

CHORUS   Easy.

MARK   Always was.

CHORUS   Beautiful.

          And then.

MARK   That weekend, the cabin, and him so sad for real. And
          it all felt like my fault. Inexplicably, even then, it felt like

my fucking fault, so I wanted to run; I wanted to bolt the doors and disconnect the phones, change my address because I couldn't, just couldn't, do it again, couldn't see him like that, and then see him leave, walk out the door again and again, and again not be able to tell him, grab him. To make him stop.

CHORUS   Make him stay.

> MARK *looks at* DAVID, *oblivious and still driving. A pause.*

MARK   The more I love you, the less I like myself. How is that possible?

> *Beat.*

CHORUS   Tell him.

MARK   What if I did. That's all I could think about. What if I just did. There in the car. What would it be like to just say it.

CHORUS   Just tell him.

MARK   Funny, I bet.

> *The* CHORUS *dissolve the car and form a moonlit balcony. Very melodramatic.*

DAVID   I'm flattered.

MARK   Flattered?

DAVID   And totally grossed out. You sure know how to shock a guy.

MARK   I've been rehearsing.

DAVID   Let's say I'm flattered, and leave it at that.

MARK   Sure.

DAVID   I don't feel the same way, of course.

MARK   Of course you don't.

DAVID   I'm not even a fag.

MARK   Of course you're not.

DAVID   I've never even thought about dudes and sex, and dude sex.

MARK   Of course you haven't. You're Pentecostal. It's immoral.

DAVID   I'm really sorry.

MARK   Thanks.

DAVID   No, I mean I feel sorry for you.

MARK   Oh. Yes.

DAVID   I'm so sorry.

MARK   Yeah.

DAVID   Sorry I'm late.

CHORUS   Pablo's.

> The CHORUS *form Pablo's.* MARK *snaps out of the fantasy.*

MARK   Late?

DAVID   My bus was late. Lost my fare. Ended up having to walk.

MARK   Didn't even notice.

DAVID   Thanks a lot.

MARK   Huh?

DAVID   You didn't even notice I was late? What planet were you on?

MARK   Sorry.

DAVID   Deep in thought?

CHORUS   Yes.

MARK   I guess.

DAVID   What is it?

CHORUS   You.

MARK   Nothing.

DAVID   Sure.

MARK   How did it go?

DAVID   It was great. Jesus, I almost forgot how much I missed that job.

MARK   Furniture got the best of you?

DAVID   Didn't even compare. I just have this need to work outdoors, you know. One shift and I feel like a million bucks.

MARK   David got a month of work at the end of summer as a lifeguard again. It was enough to make him promptly quit his job at the furniture store.

DAVID   Working outdoors.

MARK   The change in him was remarkable.

DAVID   Sunshine.

MARK   He was himself again. And all because of this job.

DAVID   The pool.

MARK   Doing what he loved.

CHORUS   As little clothing as possible.

MARK   And of course me.

DAVID   Have I ever thanked you?

MARK   For what?

DAVID   For being there. Listening to all that shit.

MARK   It wasn't shit.

DAVID   For saying it wasn't shit.

MARK   No.

DAVID   What?

MARK   I don't think you have. Thanked me.

DAVID   I haven't?

CHORUS So he did.

DAVID   You're a good friend, Mark. I don't know what I'd do without you sometimes.

MARK   Standard fare. Such niceties from my true love rarely pierced my skin anymore.

DAVID   You were there.

MARK   He thanked me.

DAVID   Thanks.

MARK   He kept thanking me.

DAVID   Thanks.

CHORUS Again and again.

DAVID   Thanks.

MARK   He tried to make it up to me.

DAVID   Mark, I want you to meet somebody.

CHORUS   Meet somebody.

DAVID   She's great. She's perfect for you.

CHORUS   She.

MARK   Oh?

DAVID   I mean, no offence, Mark, but ever since I've known you you've been in this slump. You've been moody.

MARK   Well, I've always been in that slump... I was born in that slump.

DAVID   And I think you need to get out. Meet people. You need a relationship. You'll love her.

CHORUS   Her.

MARK   I don't know.

DAVID   A lifeguard at the pool. Susan. Beautiful, smart, funny. You're perfect for each other.

CHORUS   Susan.

MARK   I don't think so.

DAVID   Oh come on. You just pop by tomorrow, check her out. You'll love her.

CHORUS   A woman!

MARK   No! I mean... look, I couldn't. She's... she's a lifeguard... and me... I'm ugly. Fat.

DAVID   What?

MARK   Yeah.

DAVID   You are not.

MARK   It's totally true. I'm repulsive; I'm huge. I was kicked out of Weight Watchers, you know.

DAVID   What?

MARK   I kept gaining weight and gaining weight—they said I was giving them a bad name.

DAVID   Funny too. See, Susan would just love that.

CHORUS   Susan.

MARK   I can't.

DAVID   Why?

CHORUS   Think fast.

MARK   I'm really busy.

DAVID   You are not busy.

MARK   Something came up.

DAVID   In the last ten seconds?

MARK   I'm in love with somebody... else.

CHORUS   Smooth.

DAVID   You're what?

MARK   I'm in love with somebody. You know. Committed.

DAVID   Since when?

MARK   Oh, it's been a while.

DAVID   How come I haven't heard this before?

MARK   You know me... private.

CHORUS   Stupid.

DAVID   Who?

CHORUS   You.

MARK   You... don't know... them... really. I mean, does anybody really know anyone? Does anybody really know themselves? I'm constantly surprising myself with stuff that I do.

DAVID   What?

MARK   I just don't think that I can start seeing somebody when I still have these feelings for... this... person... still unresolved... you know.

DAVID   This person.

MARK   Okay. I have done some pretty stupid things in my time.

CHORUS   But never...

MARK   ...never in my life have I done something as stupid as that. David Sparkes, and that expression on his face: a lopsided battle between wholehearted acceptance and complete disbelief.

CHORUS   Complete disbelief won.

DAVID   That is the stupidest thing I have heard in my life.

MARK   Wholehearted acceptance never stood a chance.

DAVID   You are in love with this person and you can't even tell me her name? Do you honestly expect me to believe this?

CHORUS   Maybe.

DAVID   I know what's going on here. You think I don't but I do.

MARK   Umm...

DAVID   I can read you like a book, I swear. You are afraid of this girl.

CHORUS   Susan.

MARK   I am?

DAVID You are afraid to meet her because of some sick desire you have to be alone and pitiful.

CHORUS Pitiful.

DAVID Stop it, Mark.

CHORUS Stop it.

DAVID It takes more guts to get out there and meet people than it does to stay home and complain about how lonely you are.

CHORUS Yeah.

DAVID You are terrified, and that's okay. Jesus, you think I'm not? You think I don't feel that way? Or everybody, or whatever, but I'll be damned if I'm going to see you give in to it.

MARK David, I—

DAVID Now you are going to come to the pool tomorrow at two and meet this girl.

CHORUS Two o'clock.

DAVID We are all going to do lunch together, and you are going to have a good time.

MARK But—

DAVID Goddammit, you are going to have lunch with this girl and have a good time even if it kills me. Later.

CHORUS   Even if it kills him.

MARK   Bye.

CHORUS   Love you.

The CHORUS *dissolve Pablo's.*

MARK   I wasn't going to go. I was going to make up some excuse. I was going to lie. I'd gotten so good at it.

DAVID   Even if it kills me.

MARK   But you were so adamant.

CHORUS   Serious.

MARK   If I didn't go, well, what then?

DAVID   Some sick desire you have to be alone and pitiful.

CHORUS   Frustration?

MARK   Suspicion?

CHORUS   Anger?

MARK   Or worse.

DAVID   How many fags does it take to screw in a light bulb?

MARK   Stop, please, just stop!

DAVID   Memory is a bitch, huh?

So is guilt.

MARK   It's my memory; you have no right to be here.

DAVID   Hey, man, I'm not here by choice. I'm just walking down the street.

MARK   I was supposed to go to lunch with the man I love, who doesn't know that I love him, and with a girl who he wanted me to love but who I could never love, and I was supposed to have a good time. No.

DAVID   Mark—

MARK   No!

Beat.

DAVID   But you came anyway.

MARK   But I came anyway.

Saying no to you was like kicking myself in the ball sack. I don't know.

DAVID   You could've just lied, Mark. You'd gotten so good at it.

CHORUS   The pool.

The CHORUS *form a swimming pool. It is backlit blue. We can see the shadows of* CHORUS *swimmers.*

DAVID   You made it.

MARK   Yeah.

DAVID   You have time for lunch?

MARK   Ah, maybe... maybe, I'm not sure.

DAVID   Well I'm all ready to go.

MARK   Just us then?

DAVID   Susan is still on until Gary gets here.

CHORUS Susan.

DAVID   Shouldn't be long now.

MARK   Great.

DAVID   What do you think?

MARK   Of what?

DAVID   Of Susan. You haven't said what you think.

MARK   That's her? In the chair?

DAVID   Nice, eh?

MARK   She's...

CHORUS A woman.

MARK   ...hot.

DAVID   And smart and funny. I think she's great for you. I think you're really going to love her.

CHORUS   Love her.

MARK   Really?

CHORUS   Love her.

DAVID   Yeah. Do you like her?

MARK   I don't know her... I haven't even met her yet.

DAVID   How she looks, man. Do you like how she looks?

CHORUS   Pressure.

MARK   I said she was hot. What do you want, a marriage licence?

DAVID   She's coming to Nicole's tomorrow night.

MARK   Oh. Great.

CHORUS   Nicole's.

DAVID   Big end-of-summer bash.

MARK   I know.

CHORUS   Nicole's.

DAVID   Nervous?

CHORUS   Terrified.

MARK   I'm fine.

DAVID   I just want you to be happy, Mark.

MARK   Look, David, I really should go, I have to—

DAVID   Yeah, relax, all right. Sue's on her way now.

CHORUS   On her way.

MARK   On her way. On her way to meet me. To eat with me. To what? What? What the hell was I doing?

CHORUS   Telling the lie.

MARK   This was wrong. This was a mistake.

CHORUS   It was all a lie.

MARK   I felt certain of that now. I felt clarity and purpose. This was a huge mistake.

DAVID   Here she comes.

CHORUS   Here she comes!

MARK   She sidled across the far end of the pool.

CHORUS   Spiky blond hair.

MARK   That blue bathing suit. Her toenails were painted. Ew.

CHORUS   Her gaze fixed.

DAVID   She sure is nice, eh?

MARK   She turned the corner and now made her way towards me. Wet footprints in her wake.

CHORUS   Her gaze fixed.

MARK   Moving towards me. And Dave.

CHORUS   Slow motion.

MARK   Children were screaming. There was a plane overhead.

CHORUS   The approach.

MARK   I wanted to be on that plane. Somebody put me on that plane!

CHORUS   The fear.

MARK   But I was trapped.

CHORUS   Nowhere to run.

MARK   She was getting closer. And closer.

CHORUS   Closing in.

MARK   Her smile grew bigger. That tight bathing suit—my god I can still see her nipples. David pushing me towards her.

CHORUS   This can't happen.

MARK   I have to get out of here.

CHORUS   Have to run.

MARK   I panicked.

MARK violently throws a chorus member who was partly out of the pool back in with a splash.

CHORUS   Help. Help me.

DAVID   Mark!

CHORUS   Help.

The CHORUS dissolve the pool.

MARK   Okay, I'm not proud, okay. I had to do it. It was the shallow end. There was a lifeguard—Susan was right there. The kid had a nose plug for Christ's sake. The complete lunacy of the situation and the potential for disaster came crashing down upon me all at once. I needed a distraction. It worked.

CHORUS   The kid was fine.

The CHORUS form a solid wall in front of which stand MARK and DAVID.

MARK   I got away.

DAVID   Mark!

MARK   But I wasn't off the hook.

DAVID   Mark, wait up.

MARK   What?

DAVID   What the hell is wrong with you?

MARK   Nothing.

DAVID   Nothing? You just threw a preschooler headfirst into a swimming pool.

MARK   It was an accident.

DAVID   What is up with you?

MARK   Nothing.

DAVID   Jesus, Mark, talk to me.

MARK   Why?

DAVID   Because I'm your friend.

MARK   I have to go.

DAVID   If you're mad at me for trying to set you up—

MARK   That's not it!

DAVID   I just wanted to make you happy. You helped me. I wanted to help you.

MARK   I appreciate that.

DAVID   But?

MARK   But I have to go.

DAVID   Wait.

MARK   See you later.

DAVID   I am so fucking tired of this, Mark! God! I am so sick and tired of trying to plot your motivation for... everything, every little thing. I mean, you obviously don't trust me. Right?

    Silence.

    I'm not stupid. I'm not. You have something... there's something on you, weighing you down. I can see it. I can see it, so. You just have to say it. You just have to tell me, Mark, because I... I'm your friend. And I can't assume anymore.

    Beat.

MARK   Later.

CHORUS   I am in love with you, fucker.

DAVID   Bye.

CHORUS   Don't go.

    The CHORUS *dissolve the wall.*

MARK   He knows.

CHORUS   He has to know.

MARK   That's what I thought. Something weighing me down? Right? That didn't come from nowhere.

CHORUS   He knows.

MARK   He had to be just waiting for me to tell him.

CHORUS   He has to know.

MARK   That day, that day I felt like throwing up. I felt like dying, for real. It was all negative, everything, everything in the world.

CHORUS   Dark and ugly.

MARK   But all I could hear in my head was your voice.

DAVID   I'm your friend. I can't assume anymore.

MARK   Your voice saying what I wanted to hear.

DAVID   I can see it. You just have to say it.

MARK   And somehow, somehow it all became really... simple. Suddenly. And clear. And easy. And obvious.

CHORUS   All of it.

DAVID   You just have to tell me.

CHORUS   He knows.

MARK   I just had to say the words.

DAVID   You just have to tell me.

> *Beat.* MARK *breaks out of the memory.*

MARK   I want to stop now.

DAVID   You can't control the ending, Mark.

MARK   This is a nice place to stop.

DAVID   You know how it ends and it's not up to you.

MARK   I was a different person then. I'm not that person anymore.

I'm not.

DAVID   It's already happened.

MARK   I want it to end here!

DAVID   See you on the other side

MARK   No!

CHORUS   You have to do this.

You have to.

> *Beat.*

Nicole's.

The CHORUS *form the interior and exterior of Nicole's house party.* MARK *and* DAVID *stand outside on the patio under the stars.*

DAVID   Hey.

MARK   Hey.

DAVID   Feeling better?

MARK   The big end-of-summer blowout. People anticipated that party for weeks. Happened every year. I thought that year was going to be the best.

DAVID   I wasn't sure you would come.

MARK   Wouldn't miss it. Biggest party of the year.

DAVID   My first one. I feel kinda left out.

MARK   You weren't here last year?

DAVID   This time last year I was looking for a job. In a furniture store. Remember?

MARK   That was a year ago.

DAVID   Happy birthday.

MARK   I'm sorry about before. The pool.

DAVID   Yeah.

MARK   You were right. About everything. There is something on me... bothering me. I guess I just have to get over it and get on with it, right?

DAVID   If you can, yeah.

MARK   It's been on my mind for some time now. And it wasn't until you talked to me the other day that I realized it was okay. That I was being silly. I do trust you.

DAVID   I'm glad to hear that.

         MARK *gets upset.*

         Hey. Don't.

MARK   Jesus... I'm sorry... it's... it's just so hard to... fuck, I can't say it, you know?

DAVID   You don't have to.

MARK   No, I think I do.

DAVID   You admitted it to yourself. That's enough.

MARK   I want to feel good again, Dave. I want to—

DAVID   Well, this is where you start. She's here.

> MARK *stares at him, crushed.*

Susan. She was a bit ruffled by what happened at the pool. But she likes you. Noticed you. How could she not, right? You made an impression. She thinks you're cute, her words. Wants to meet you.

MARK   She's… here.

DAVID   And I think that this self-esteem problem, whatever it is that you have been having, this ego-bashing that's been weighing you down, needs someone else to kill it. To show you what you're worth.

MARK   Self-esteem problem.

DAVID   So she's here. You're feeling better. Have fun, man.

MARK   Excuse me.

DAVID   Where are you going? Mark! Mark!

CHORUS   Stupid!

> *The* CHORUS *dissolve Nicole's and form a maze of hands and faces that* MARK *has to pick his way through. He*

eventually lands centre stage as the CHORUS *form a small bedroom.* DAVID *bursts in behind him.*

DAVID Mark.

> DAVID *attempts to stop* MARK *from leaving. Their physical exchange becomes almost violent as* MARK *attempts to get past him. In frustration* DAVID *grabs* MARK *hard by the shoulders, which leads very quickly to a heated near kiss.* DAVID *stops slowly as he realizes what he has done.* MARK *is quietly in shock.*

DAVID I'm sorry. Sorry about that, I...

> DAVID *retreats a little. There is a small, uncomfortable pause.*

I'm just drunk, I think. I'm...

No.

No, I'm not. I'm not drunk.

Mark, I...

> *The* CHORUS, *beginning to giggle softly and unseen by* DAVID *and* MARK, *enter outside the room with a birthday cake.*

CHORUS David, come on, we got it.

Shut up, he'll hear you.

> DAVID *looks at* MARK, *conflicted.*

DAVID   Listen. Ah, I have to... don't go, okay...

CHORUS   David, could you come out here for a second?

DAVID   Yeah, sure, Nicole, I'll be right out.

DAVID turns back to MARK.

Don't go... just... I'll be right back.

Please.

After DAVID leaves, the CHORUS giggling grows as they storm the room in preparation for the birthday surprise. MARK is messed up, confused by it all, paranoid, trying to cover and recover.

MARK   What's going on? What's... You hear that? Did you hear what just happened in there? David Sparkes. I know, eh, who knew. But I suppose you can't tell by just looking at 'em. I never could anyway. No lisp, see, that threw me off. They're sneaky now, you can't even tell anymore. Yeah. Hey, hey, listen how many fags can you fit on a bar stool? How many? No, listen. Whatever, man, listen! How many fucking fags can you fit on a bar stool? How many fags can you...!? The answer is three, three but you got to...

In reaction to this, the CHORUS has been slowly leaving the room. Once they are all gone MARK can finally see DAVID standing with the glowing birthday cake. He has heard everything MARK has just said. They stare at each other for a moment.

A long silence. DAVID *silently walks away.*

Dave.

David.

Stop!

> DAVID *stops. He slowly turns and looks at* MARK. *Silence.*

DAVID You didn't say that. And it's too late to say it now.

> *Beat.*

Why didn't you stop me then?

Why didn't you come after me?

MARK I couldn't.

DAVID Why not?

> *Beat.*

Did you hate yourself that much?

You shouldn't have. You're all right.

MARK Thanks.

> *Beat.*

DAVID I gotta go.

MARK   Yup.

DAVID   No, I mean I gotta go. You got to let me. For real.

> MARK *snaps his fingers.* DAVID *doesn't disappear.* MARK *shrugs.*

It's been four years.

MARK   So what do I do? Tell me exactly how I am supposed to do that.

> *Beat.*

I heard somewhere that you moved away. That night was the last time I saw you.

> DAVID *leaves. The* CHORUS *dissolve the bedroom and retreat upstage. Silence for a moment.* MARK *is very much alone.*

But then there was Thanksgiving and Christmas, and Easter, and my new job, and Mom's cancer scare, and that fall on the Eurorail, and Francois, and his patience. And then truth finally, and Mom, and the fighting. The endless fighting, and then the end of the fighting. And then Johnny with the sad eyes and his fucked-up family and Charlie, ah Charlie, and those thirteen months when I truly felt that I had met my match, and the subsequent three when I swore off men. Four years that got progressively shorter, progressively easier. And then there was today.

MARK and DAVID walk towards each other from opposite sides of the stage, like at the beginning.

Today, when there was nothing wrong, and everything was right, and I was walking and happy, for the first time in a long time, and then there was you.

MARK and DAVID meet each other centre stage and stop like at the beginning. MARK stares at DAVID during the following, while DAVID looks at the ground.

And you're right here in front of me, and it all comes flooding back. Stuff I thought I killed a long time ago. And every part of me has a voice.

DAVID looks up at him. Throughout the following, individual CHORUS members move one by one downstage to form a solid wall behind DAVID and MARK.

The sad part. The happy part. Parts that only want to sleep. Parts that feel nothing but anger. And regret. And they all, every part of me, wants to scream at you. To tell you the truth. Tell you that I fucked up. Tell you that I'm an asshole in such an incredibly beautiful way that you couldn't possibly agree. Tell you everything necessary to make me the brightest star in your sky again. But I can't. Because I know I'm not. Because I don't deserve to be. And so all I can say is... hey.

DAVID drops his eyes from him and begins to walk away.

Because I can't control the ending.

DAVID stops at the end of the stage. Both of them with their backs to each other. MARK is oblivious, but there is a pause of suspension and hope. Finally...

DAVID   Hey.

He turns to look at MARK. The lights go out as MARK spins to look at him and there is a collective gasp from the CHORUS.

Robert Chafe was born in St. John's, where he currently works as Artistic Director and playwright for Artistic Fraud of Newfoundland. He is the author of numerous plays, including *Oil & Water*; *Afterimage*, which won the Governor General's Literary Award for Drama in 2010; and *Butler's Marsh* and *Tempting Providence*, which were shortlisted in 2004 for the Governor General's Literary Award.

First edition: September 2014
Printed and bound in Canada by Marquis Book Printers, Montreal

Cover photo of Ron Klappholz provided courtesy of Peter Bromley
and Artistic Fraud of Newfoundland.

Cover design by BFdesign.

All interior photos provided courtesy of Peter Bromley and Artistic
Fraud of Newfoundland and feature Brad Bonnell, Petrina Bromley,
Courtney Brown, Robert Chafe, Greg Gale, Victoria Harnett,
Marie Jones, Willow Kean, Ron Klappholz, Justin Nurse, Mark
Power, Michael Power, Anna Stassis, Jeremy Wells, Mark White,
and Alison Woolridge.

PLAYWRIGHTS
CANADA PRESS
202-269 Richmond Street West
Toronto, ON
M5V 1X1

416.703.0013
info@playwrightscanada.com
playwrightscanada.com

RECYCLED
Paper made from
recycled material
FSC® C103567